PIAZZA ARMERINA

THE MOSAICS OF
VILLA ROMANA DEL CASALE
AND MORGANTINA

CONTENTS

agnificent town of Enna province, situated on three hills about 700 meters above
a, rich of charm not only for the now famous Villa Romana del Casale and its mosa-
, but also for its monuments and its beautiful urban plan shared as a "fishbone",
ry aparent in the Monte District dating from the Norman period. Piazza, (the ad-
tive Armerina was added in 1882) is located on the western edge of the old Val
Noto, between the plains of Gela and the Erei mountains, the mountains chain of
ntral Sicily.

Today the town has about 22.000 inhabitants over an area about 303 sq. km., ri
of woods and parks, suitabile for walks.
Its ancient origins, dating back to the VIII-VII sec.B.C., are confirmed by artifac
dating back to greek colonization, found on Monte Rossomanno on Monte Navo
and especially on the Mountain of Marzo. The Roman period was also brilliant,
witnessed by the presence of the beautiful Villa del Casale, who has received the re
ognition by "Unesco Heritage", as "inalienable heritage for humanity".
Piazza Armerina had its best period in the Middle Ages and precisely during the Nc
man domination, when it was colonized by settlers from Lombardy, who have left
legacy of a dialect of Gaul-Italic roots.
Piazza Armerina was built and on the hill Armerino, and was destroyed in 1161
Guglielmo II for hosting elements opposed to the Norman King and then rebuilt
Gugliemo II n the Mira hill, the current quarter "Monte". The city soon resumed
growth and became an important political center and in 1296 the Parlament of Sic
that elected king Frederic II of Aragon who promulgated the "custom of the towr
was convened there. This custom are still part of the "Book of Privileges" stored
the Central Library.
The prestige of Piazza Armerina also grew with the arrival of new religious orde
and military, as the Knights of the Holy Sepulchre, the Templars and Hospitaller
Other groups of people from the mainland also moved to Piazza Armerina. To acc
modate the increased population the wall perimeter was enlarged.
Some remains of these walls are still found in the Castellina District.

Architectural perspective of the Cathedral of the Renaissance Baroque style.

Piazza Armerina night view.

n 1348 there was also a pandemic plague which decimated the population. It seems hat on this occasion the banner of Our Lady of Victories was found, which later be-ame the patron saint of the city.

Piazza Armerina view day.

In the successive centuries there were moments of expansion and crisis, especially when some feudal obtained permission to cultivate contiguos hamlets such as Valguarnera, San Michele of Ganzeria, Niscemi and San Cono.

Despite these events, the city was placed in charge of a "comarca" which included six neighbouring fiefs. During this period magnificent palaces, churches, convents and a hospital was built that Piazza Armerina was nicknamed "opulent city" by the Emperor Charles V. However several noble families moved to both Palermo and Naples, that were the locations of the royal courts ok the Kindom, the slow decline of Piazza Armerina set in.

In 1817, thanks to its prestige as a important city, obtained permission to become seat to a new diocese and was appointed as capuital of an administrative district in the new province of Caltanissetta.

During the First World War, General A. Cascino was awanted a gold medal to the military valour, and his monument stands in the square named at him. Finally, when in 1926 Catanissetta was preferred to Piazza Armerina to become one of the seven newly established provinces, all the aspirations to regain the role of centrality of the area which Piazza Armerina had for several centuries collapsed.

The visit of Villa Romana del Casale, wich on its own is worth a trip to Piazza Armerina, is one of the most important monuments of the Roman world's and was declared in 1997 "Unesco Heritage".

This beautiful and great imperial villa with mosaic floors covering an area of 3.500 square meters., is the most important evidence of Roman civilization in Sicily and in Italy.

The villa, built in the III and IV century A.D. by some rich landowner of the time, or even by the Roman Emperor Maximianus Herculius, included a large set of rooms, about 60, with different functions, and arranged on four levels, which follows configuration of the ground.

The initial building, perhaps an originally much simpler villa, of the second century A.C. was expanded in later centuries, and it turned into a country residence of some roman nobles.

The villa was part of one of the many estates, where large Roman aristocrats landowners, procuratores using slave labour, devoted themselves to the land use and enjoyment of leisure provided by the fertile countryside of Sicily.

This villa, which stood at the foot of Mount Mangone, in the valley of the river Gela that along with other sources of water supplyed the spa, satisfed the needs of th villa and allowed irrigation of the fields, stood near the Statio Philosophiana, a sto and change horses, located along the Antonine Itinerary, which connected Catania t Agrigento.

It seems that the name Philosophiana, alluded to the cultural interests of the owner as demonstrated by some figures of the mosaics.

This hypothesis has led some historians to think that the owner of the Villa could b an aristocratic landowners near the imperial court, such as Rufo Volusiano or Procul Populonio or a consul or prefect, rather than the emperor Maximian. The emperor who was from Pannonia and was of humble origins, thanks to his skills as a genera had been granted the coreggente Emperor Diocleziano, who had placed him unde the protection of Hercules, from which the name Herculius (in the villa there are nu merous mosaics that refer to Hercules, the great mythological hero).

Thanks to his victories, Massimiano was proclaimed emperor on 1 April 286 A.D. an was Augustus Emperor until 306, when he abdicated in Milan to retire to private life Massimiano lived during the historical period of Tetrarchy, which was instituted b the Roman Emperor Gaius Valerius Diocleziano, when he realised that on his ow could not sustain the empire, whose government was then entrusted to four people two Augusti and two Caesars.

The two Augusti were Diocleziano, who kept for himself the empire of the East an Massimiano who held the part of the empire to the West with capital Milan.

The two Augusti then appointed two Caesars, who were respectively Galerio e Cos tanzo Cloro.

With the death of Costanzo Clorio there was a stringgle for until that came to powe the popular Constantino, who defeated at Ponte Milvio Massenzio, became sole em peror and established his residence at Byzantium, which became known as Constan tinople. Constantine in 313 A.D., proclaimed freedom of worship for the Christian: and it is in this period that lies the realization of the Villa Romana del Casale.

The style, the hairstyle that the headgear of some figures represented in the mosaics indicate that were created in III century A.D. and are certainly the work of Africar craftmen, given that the mosaics are comparable to some founded in Tunisia anc Algeria. Also the colorful pieces are from North Africa, the area around Carthage, a that time, the cultural vanguard of the Western Roman Empire.

The story of this villa is very interesting. After the end of the Roman empire, with the arrival of the Visigoths and Vandals, the villa was definitely plundered, but wher Belisarius defeated barbarians, the dwelling was inhabited again as suggesting some restoration walls. For several centuries it was inhabited by the Byzantines, who ir turn were expelled by the Saracens when they conquered Sicily in 827.

The villa was inhabited again, so that this area for some time was called Casale de Saraceni.

The new lords, the Normans continued to live in the Villa, until a landslide from Monte Mangone cover the whole Villa with a mudslide, somehow protecting it for several centuries, but also making it inaccessably to the point that even local people lost a track of the Villa.

The Villa is mentioned again in a chroniche of Piazza of 1640, where there is a reference precisely to Casale dei Saraceni. The Villa was the subject of clandestine excavations for many years, until 1881, when the archaeologist Pappalardo, commissioned by the municipality began a regular series of excavations, which led to the discovery of the floor of triclinum, where the Labours of Hercules were represented.

The works continued with Paolo Orsi in the late 1920s and only since 1950s, the Superintendent of Syracuse with L. Bernabo Brea began a real scientific excavation. This operation, conducted by Professor V. Gentile, assisted by local experts, has allowed to rediscover in about ten years, the noble part of the house with precious mosaics. Many rooms, such as the servants' rooms, stables and warehouses still remain to be discovered.

In 1970, designed by the architect Minissi, a plexiglass canopy was made to protect the mosaics that could be visited only after the recent restoration in 2008. It is noticeable tha African workers used small pieces for animals (opus verniculatum), larger pieces for geometric designs (opus tesselatum), and finally, pieces of marble for the basilica, (opus sectile).

VISIT OF THE VILLA

Since the villa built on the slopes of Monte Mangone,
it presents characteristics of terraced buildings.

THERE ARE THREE POSSIBLE ROUTES
to enjoy the visit of the Villa:

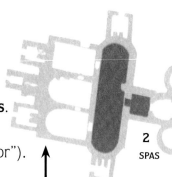

PC

ON THE FIRST LEVEL ARE:

2)   Spas

2A) Poligonal courtyard with the **arcade** and then
the **Kiosk of Venus** and the **vestibule of the Baths**.

3)   Latrine.

7)   Gymnasium, and the **Entrance of Villa** ("corridor").

ON THE SECOND LEVEL ARE:

4)   Vestibule of the villa or *aditus*.

5-6) Peristylium with a large fountain
in the center and the "lararium"
with the big "quadrangle",
the **little latrine**.

8)   Trapezoidal vestibule.

9-10-11-12) Guest rooms and those of the
servants (from 8 and contiguous).

16) Room of Orpheus, the **corridor
linking** the triclinium with *xystus*
(arcade and hallway) and the **kitchen
of triclinium** (near the corridor).

THE THIRD LEVEL ARE:

The apartments of the masters, **Dominus and Domina**:

13) Corridor of the great hunt.

19-20-21) Apartments of the family of the landowner.

22) Private latrine.

17) Classroom basilica and the **Triclinio** with classroom triloba.

18) Xystus.

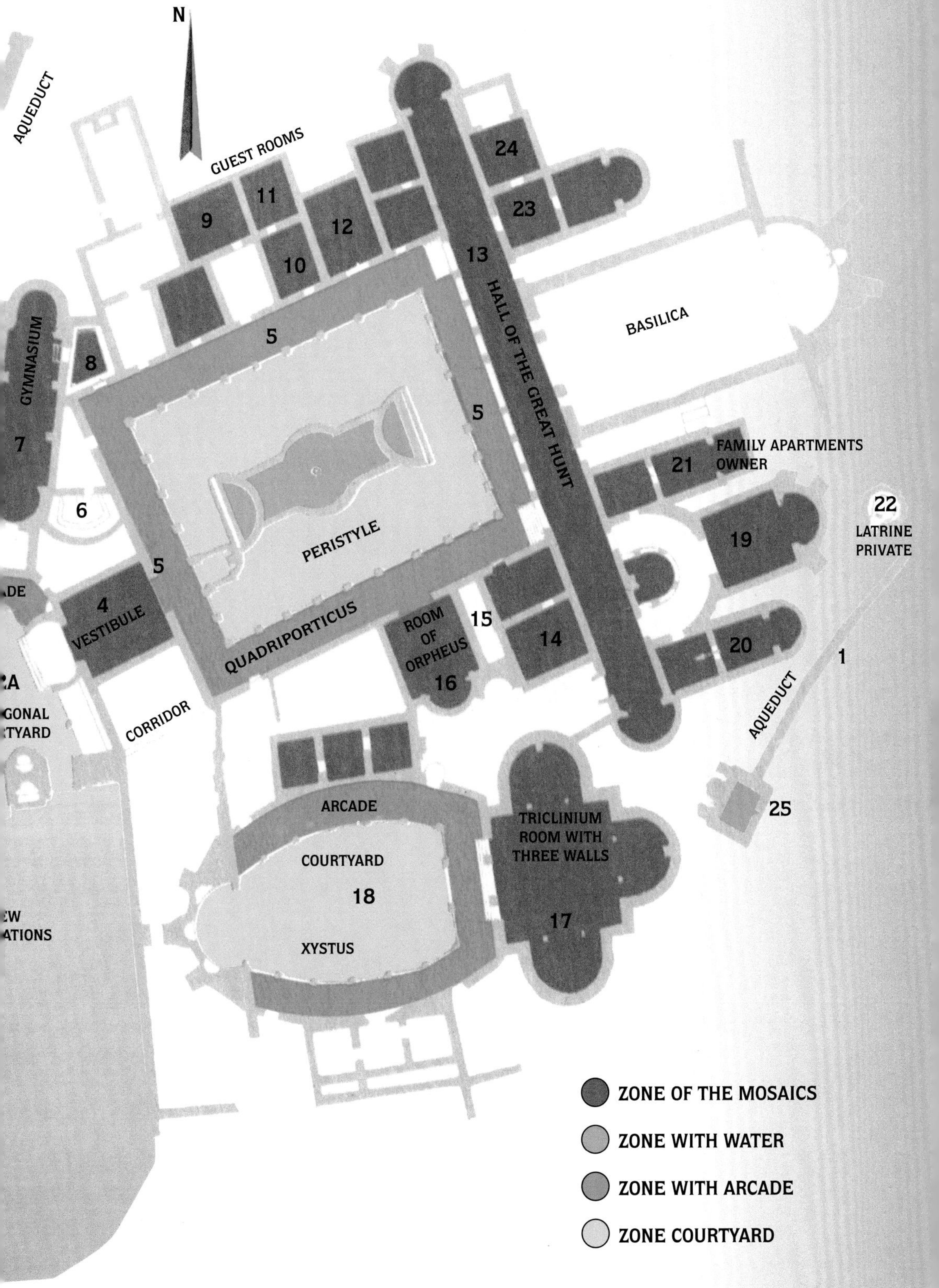

N

AQUEDUCT

GUEST ROOMS

24

11

23

9

12

10

13

5

BASILICA

GYMNASIUM

8

5

13

5

7

5

FAMILY APARTMENTS
OWNER

6

21

22
LATRINE
PRIVATE

19

5

PERISTYLE

DE

4 VESTIBULE

QUADRIPORTICUS

ROOM
OF
ORPHEUS

15

20

1

14

RA

GONAL
TYARD

CORRIDOR

16

AQUEDUCT

25

ARCADE

COURTYARD

18

TRICLINIUM
ROOM WITH
THREE WALLS

EW
ATIONS

XYSTUS

17

⬤ ZONE OF THE MOSAICS

⬤ ZONE WITH WATER

⬤ ZONE WITH ARCADE

◯ ZONE COURTYARD

FIRST ITINERARY: THE SPAS

Entering the current entry, you encounter the first Roman aqueduct that remind
us of the largest in Rome. Then we arrive at the spa made up of several parts with
different functions: *prefurnium*, *steam bath*, *tepidarium*, ointments hall, *frigidarium*
and gym.

The "**PRAEFURNIUM**" is a set of three furnaces that heated the water, which, placed
in a large bathtub, through terratocca pipes was carried in *calidarium*.

Terracotta pipes were used, because they were not subject to expansion as a refractory material, therefore preventing the walls of the furnace from bursting.

The **CALIDARIUM**, or room of the hot baths was divided into several areas, which
allowed the separation of the men from the women. The internal temperature wa
regulated by windows and valves placed on roofs.

Tepidarium.

Moreover a **FOUNTAIN** (labrum), ensured a little bit fresh air in that overheated room. The central room, with the the floor suspended on terracotta bricks for the circulation of hot air, was used as a sauna (laconicum). In the walls the tubules can still be seen, which allowed hot air to circulate.

The function of lowering the body temperature after the sauna, was carried in the next room called "**TEPIDARIUM**".

Terracotta pipes (refractory material) of Prefurnium.

It was a room with double apse and raisened floor allow the circulation of the hot steam.

In this room, the mosaics are almost gone, but it is assumed that there was represented the race of the torches (*lampadedromia*).

Remains of Roman aqueduct potter arches that led water directly to the pool.

The next room is that of **MASSAGE**, where guests were massaged and anointed with oil. In the mosaic on the floor one can see two slaves, one with a bucket in one hand, and the other with a broom, and girded with a strip that shows their name: **Cassi and Tito**.

This room, that presents perhaps restorations of peraphs the Byzantine period, lead to the next room, that of "**frigidarium**", the room of the cold baths.

This is an octagonal room with side niches, four of which served as changing room (*apodyterium*).

We assume that once they were equipped with benches on which clothing and towel were laid, and two were used as entrance for the gymnasium and the room of oint ments, and the other two swimming pools, a larger one, which received water from the river Gela, and another smaller one for warm baths.

In the central hall there is a scene with Nereids, dolphins, cherubs fishermen, newt and sea lions. In the niches are represented two beautiful scenes: one with the girl in the act undressing helped by two maids, and the other a man sitting on a stool on leopard skin, aided by two servants who hand him the clothes.

Partial view of the spas - frigidarium.

Frigidarium room massage. Servants helping their master to undress.

Hall of anointing where guests were massaged and anointed with oil.

Frigidarium - Central hall, the scene of the great mosaic is explicitly aquatic
and represens Nereids, dolphins, cherubs fishermen, newts and sea lions

After the visit to the spa you can visit the large latrine, the courtyard polygonal and the kiosk of Venus.

The **LARGE LATRINE**, located in the spa, had a small entrance and consisted of a semicircular part where the seats with a central hole were placed, now missing, and it was certainly covered by curtains supported by columns, of which only remnants can be seen.

In the channel water continuosly flew to take the wastewater to the river Gela. Nearby is the **KIOSK OF VENUS**, taking its name from the fragments of a statue of Venus found there. This is a very small room, which served as the servants' entrance to the spas complex. There are mosaics in geometric designs, typical of servitude.

Polygonal courtyard, the great hall with eleven columns with Ionic capital which represented the entrance of the large vil

Large latrine.

Attached to this room is the **VESTIBULE OF THE BATHS**, consisting of a square room with frescoed walls and with floors with very elaborate and hight quality mosaics.

From Venus kiosk you enter the **POLYGONAL COURTYARD**, a large hall with eleven columns with Ionic capitals, which represented the entrance to the large villa. The archade has remains of a mosaic geometric scales, while in the center of the courtyard are the remains of a square fountain, which had the function ofcollecting rainwater (*impluvium*), which was in turn conveyed to the nearby large latrine. The entrance consisted of three large huge arches, the largest of which was the central of 4.50 meters.

At the pylons were four niches that once contained statues, and there are also four basins that served as nymphs, two rectangular and two shaped as shells.

On the outside of the pylons are still traces of frescoes, where there is still a military emblem (*Signum*), with the effigies of our tetrarchs inside medallions.

This finding would suggest that the villa belonged to the Emperor Massimiano.

Mosaic floor of the vestibule of the baths.

SECOND ITINERARY: THE GUESTS ROOMS

After the forecourt a few steps lead to the second level of the villa which allowed to observe from above the various rooms for the guests.

The entrance to the villa was truly monumental, with three arches that recall the triumphal arches of the Emperors which are the doors sill and the front doors and the holes on the of the gates.

In the large **hall** there are several columns with Ionic capitals that once supported a roof with compluvium the middle at the floor, where is the base of the square fountain, which collected rainwater and flew it to the large latrine.

The visit starts with the **entrance** (*aditus*), which represents the mosaic of people with chandeliers and bay leaves, welcome the owner or any famous guests.

This room leads to

Top: Entrance (aditus), the mosaic represents people, with chandeliers and bay leaves who welcome the Master or any famous guests.

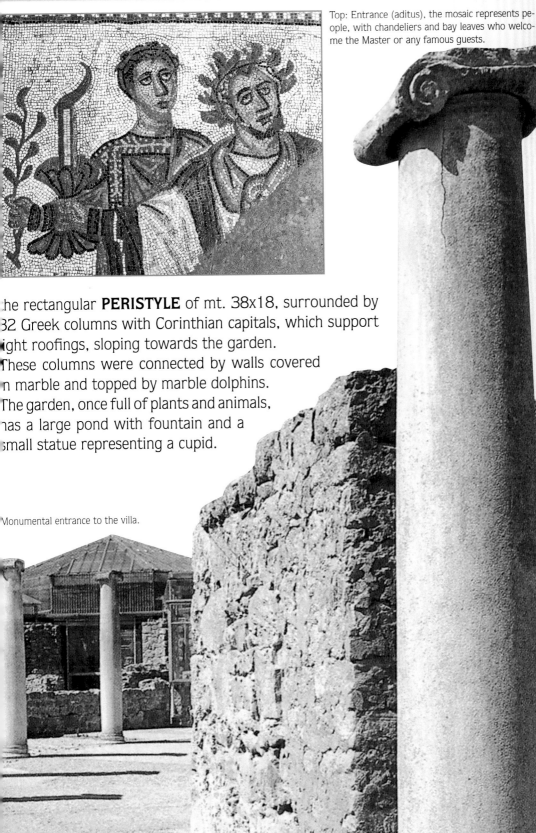

he rectangular **PERISTYLE** of mt. 38x18, surrounded by 32 Greek columns with Corinthian capitals, which support ight roofings, sloping towards the garden.
These columns were connected by walls covered n marble and topped by marble dolphins.
The garden, once full of plants and animals, has a large pond with fountain and a small statue representing a cupid.

Monumental entrance to the villa.

Peristyle rectangular 38x18 meters, surrounded by 32 Greek columns with Corinthian capitals.
The garden, once full of plants and animals, has a large pond with fountain and a small statue of a cupid.

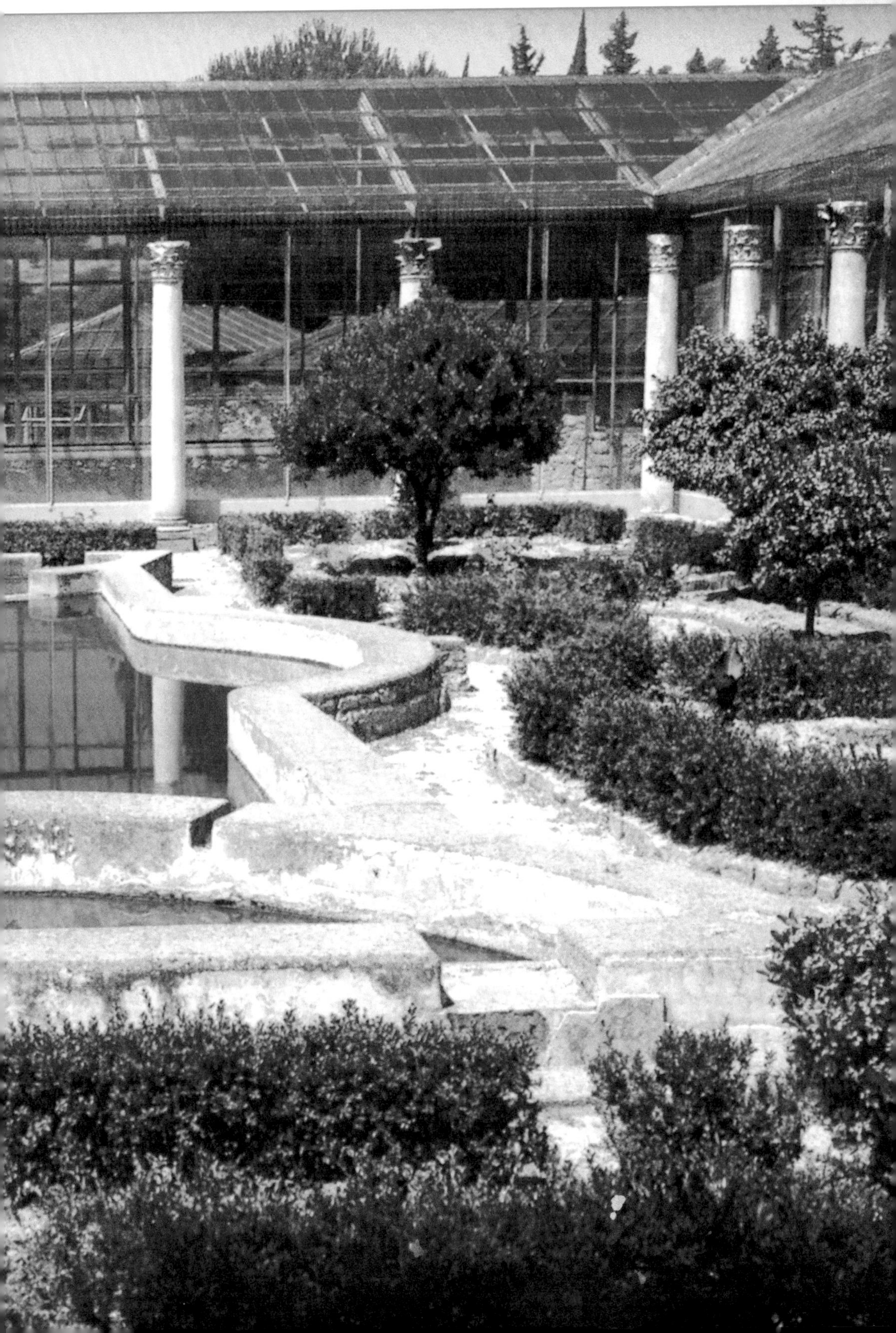

The mosaics of the floor of the archade are 162 heads of animals, both wild and domestic, and birds, framed in wreaths of laurel.

The successive room is the small **LATRINE**, that was destined for the guests of the villa. Today have been rebuilt a few seats in cement (the originals were of marble) with a channel in which water flowed continuously.

At the right there is a bowl that rather than a bowl for washing, it seems that i served to fuel the drain for the seats.

The mosaics floors represent animals in a race: a leopard, a partridge, a hare, a ot tarda, and a onager.

Holes can still be seen for the jambs of a door which guaranteed a certain intimacy.

Along the way you come to the **GYMNASIUM** (*gymnasium*), a rectangular room with two apses, where the guests warmed up the muscles before entering the spas

The mosaics of the gym represent the race of chariots, which were held in the Circus Massimo in honor of the goddess Ceres, whose cult was deeply felt in this part of Sicily. The four factions that were vying for the prize were distinguished by the clothes of different colours of charioteers: green (*prasina*), white (*albata*), blue (*veneta*) and red (*russata*).

The arena was divided into two parts by a *central spine* with at the ends the goals, consisting of bronze columns. From right to left you notice a Winged Victory over a column, a building (*phala*) from where the privileged spectators could watch the race, the obelisk of Augustus (this has led to speculations about the ownershpof the villa), the goddess Cibele (*Magna Mater*) on Leon, the segnagiri (*ovaria*).

uriously but also an indication of the precision with which the work was performed, he ovaria has four eggs lowered, indicating that the race was halfway through, as vere made in all eight laps.

)ne could also note the scene of the clothing of a charioteer and the twelve gates *carceres*), from which emerged the quadrighe.

)n th other side of the arena are represented, the scene of the presentation of the)uadriga award winner, announced by the end of the race *tybicen*, a judge sounding long tube and a clash between two chariots, one of which is overturning.

hese realistic detalis, evident even in the charioteers urging their horses to the race, vere noticed and appreciated by the *dominus* of the villa, when he came into the rapezoidal room to go to the spas.

The small latrine, which was intended for guests of the villa.

Scene of the Quadriga award winner, announced by the end of the race tybicen, the judge who plays a long tube.

n the scene there is Eutropia, the wife of Dominus Massimiano, accompanying their children, Massenzio and Fausta, with two maids, one carrying clothes to wear after the bath, the other one a box with oil for the bath.

Througt this **VESTIBULE TRAPEZOIDAL** the owner of the villa and his guests went to the spa. It appears that the bench covered with slabs of limestone present in the hall allowed to sit for those waiting to enter the spa.

The walls were coloured frescoes. It seems that the mosaics of the floor represented Eutropia, the wife of *dominus* Massimiano, while accompanying their children, Massenzio and Fausta, with two maids, one preparing clothes to wear after the bath, the other a box with oils for the bath. One interesting detail are the eyes of Massenzio, realized with a triangular piece and the other with a square piece to highlight the strabismus of which he was afflicted. Perfectionism of mosaic appears is highlighted by the shadows of the figures, drawn with black stripes at the feet and by the hair of the *domina*, coiffereud, in the fashion of the time, and then by the rich garments, from earrings and necklace.

Temples dedicated to Jupiter, Roma and Hercules.

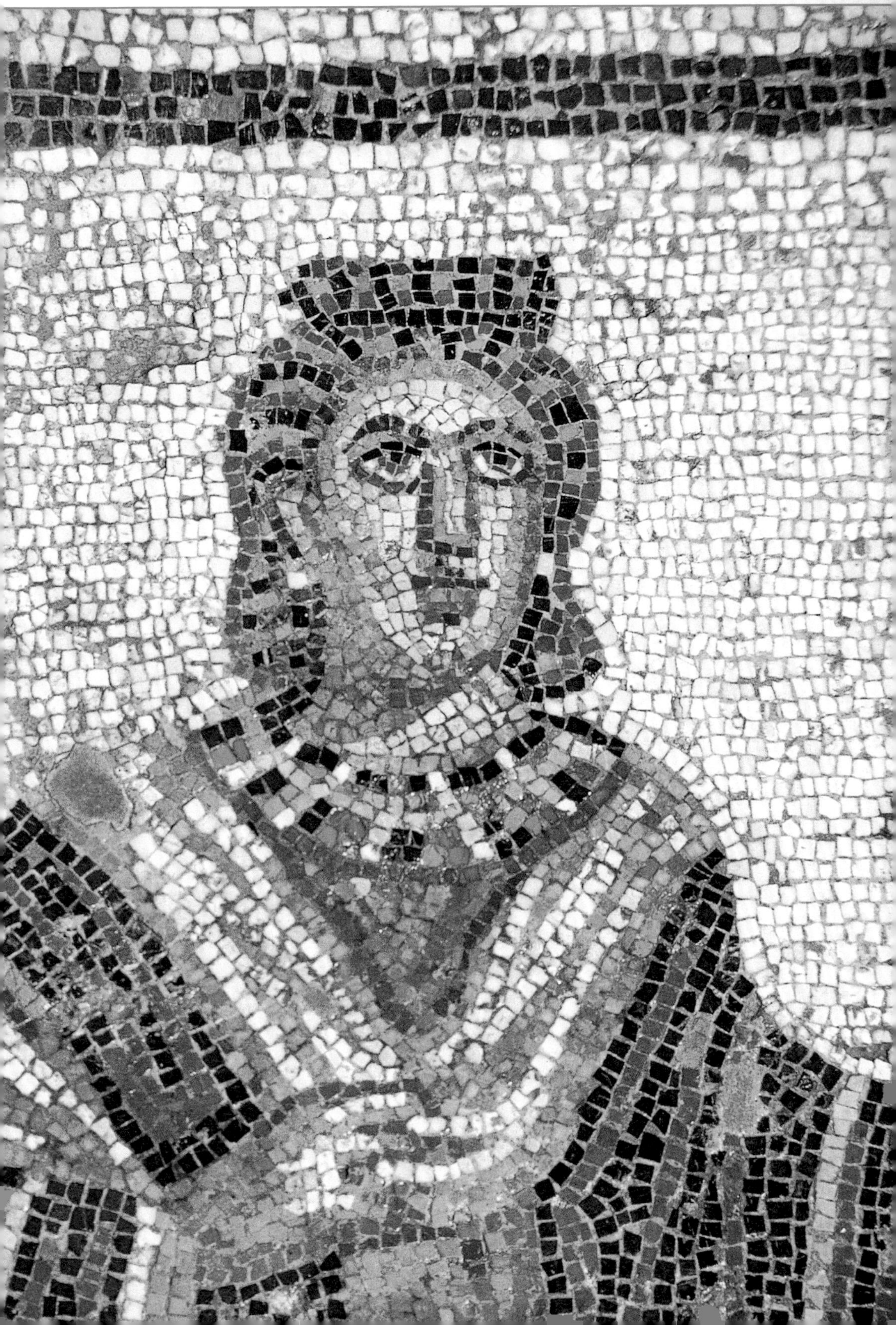

Detail of the **room of the dance** - A young man lift up a young girl.

From here there are the rooms for the servants and the guests, very simple and with mosaic with geometric designs: the **ROOM OF THE OVEN**, where peraphs during the Arabic period an oven was built to bake the pottery.

In the **INTERMEDIATE ROOM**, dedicated to personnel service, where there are mosaics with geometric designs, stars, squares and hexagons. Next there are other

Room of the dance - Particular of a girl, dancing, raises a red veil over her head.

ooms and a kitchen, all very simple and with mosaic with larges pieces.
Next the **ROOM OF THE DANCE**, a rectangular room used as a bedroom for the
guests, with frescoes on the walls and mosaics on the floor, depicting a girl who
dances, raises a red veil over her head, while a young man lift up a girl. For some this
ould be a representati of The rape of the Sabines.

The adjoining room, called the **FOUR SEASONS**, served as a vestibule perhaps for the guests. The mosaics are, within four medallions, representation of the **four seasons**. In the **spring** a young woman is represented with roses on her head.

Mosaics of the room of the four seasons.

n the **summer** a young man with ears of corn in his head.
n the **autumn** one Girl with grapes on her head. In the **winter** a young man with his
head adorned with leaves and a coat. Next to the seasons there are also birds and fish.

The next room, the **ROOM OF EROTIC** (Cupids) **fishermen** is supposed to have been the *triclinium* or dining room for the guests.
The mosaic pavement represents the cupids intent to fish in a rich sea of fish.
The different scenes also describe four different ways of fishing: net, fishingine, harpoon and fish traps.
In the upper part of the scene is the background of a large villa with exedra and long colonnade.

First register - Two servants who lead and releas two dogs.

Second register - A propitiatory sacrifice to Diana.

n the north part of the peristyle is the **ROOM OF THE LITTLE HUNTING**, a ectangular room perhaps used for the guests to stay, where some scenes represent various phases of hunting that took place in the countryside surrounding the villa. From top to bottom, the hunting scene is divided into **five registers**.

n **the first Register** (above) you can see two servants who lead and released two dogs in the countryside where they will hunt.

The second Register (the center) shows the atoning sacrifice to Diana, represented on an altar with a bow and quiver. In this scene, scholars want to see on the left Costanzo Cloro, the Caesar massimiano, to behind his son Costantino, the future emperor, and on the right the son Massimino.

The third register shows, the left, two hunters who hunt with a falcon, while peering two thrushes. In the middle there are two hunters who feast under a suspended red curtain suspended, while the slaves wait them.

n **the fourth Register** a dog bites a hare, on the right a hunter hit a hiding hate in a bush. Below, finally, on the left two riders push the deer into a net and on the right a wild boar wounded by a hunting spear attacks a hunter who is rescue by his fellow huntsmen.

Finally, perhaps allocated to servants, we find the **ROOM OF THE SQUARE DESIGN** and the **GEOMETRIC DESIGNS**.

Third register - Two hunters who hunt with a falcon while peering two thrushes.

Second register - A propitiatory sacrifice to Diana.

Third register - Two hunters feast under the suspended red curtain, while the slaves wait them.

Fourth - A wild boar wounded on a hunting spear attacks an hunter.

Fourth - A hunter hits a hiding hare in a bush.

Fourth - Two riders push the deer into the net.

THIRD ITINERARY: THE PRIVATE APARTMENTS

The **AMBULATORY OF THE GREAT HUNTING**, more than 60 metres long, perforr the role of function rooms for the *dominus*, *domina* and their children, in additic to the basilica and the triclinium. This is the room with the most beautiful mosaic: which represent the phases of hunting, with scenes of the capture of wild anima and spectacular sceneries.

The ambulatory has at its ends two exedras, with magnificent mosaics of female fig ures who personify the most distant provinces of Rome, Mauritania and India.

In the central part is Italy, where the wild animals will be used for circences games On the left are represented scenes from the capture of exotic wild animals: panther: antelope, wild horses, lions and boars. The scenes take place in an African landscap with palm trees, hills, trees, houses and buildings with archade. All captured anima are loaded onto carts pulled by oxen and in turn loaded onto ships in the port c Carthage. The capture of wild animals, is witnessed by a noble person flanked by tw

The ambulatory of the great hun

The Arab phoenix.

soldiers with shields, that carries a cylindrical headgear and someone identifies with Massimiano.

In the central part of the mosaic is landing of the beasts at Ostia, where two officials, with control sticks in hand, supervise the operation.

In the terminal part of the ambulatory are represented scenes of the capture of tigers, a lion killing a donkey and the capture of a mythological winged griffin. But this scene is also open to other interpretations. In the exedra terminating the ambulatory, is represented **India**, personified by a female figure with dark skin and that has in her hand a tusk of ivory. On her left is an elephant and on her right hand a tiger.

Above the elephant is represented **Arab phoenix**, the bird that burned and died and after three days was reborn from ashes.

Personification of India.

The capture of the buffalo, the tiger and the antelope.

Various moments of great hunting.

Leopard attacking an antelope.

Lion devouring an antelope.

Panther bites the antelope.

The capture of the rhinoceros.

A group of hunters capture the tiger.

Two hunters carry the warthog captured.

The capture of ostriches.

The hunters are ready to catch the panthers.

A wagon pulled by oxen loaded with booty goes to the point of embarkation.

The trapped animals are transported on the barres.

Two hunters with a shield intent to launch a deadly dart on its prey.

The capture of mithologic winged griffin.

The tiger shows her maternal love helping her cubs.

The transport of prey.

All animals are loaded on ships in the port of Carthage.

ROOM OF THE TEN GIRLS IN BIKINIS

On the right are two of the ambulatory environments, perhaps for the servants of *dominia*.

The first has mosaic floors with geometric patterns and remains of frescoes on the walls.

The second is the famous **room of ten girls in bikinis**.

This room has a double floor, a sign that at some point in time the room changed destination, becoming the gym for the daughters of the *dominus*.

The girls are represented with **subligar** (panties) and **stropkion** and are engaged in various sports disciplines.

The game with weights.

The discus throwing.

The discipline of the race.

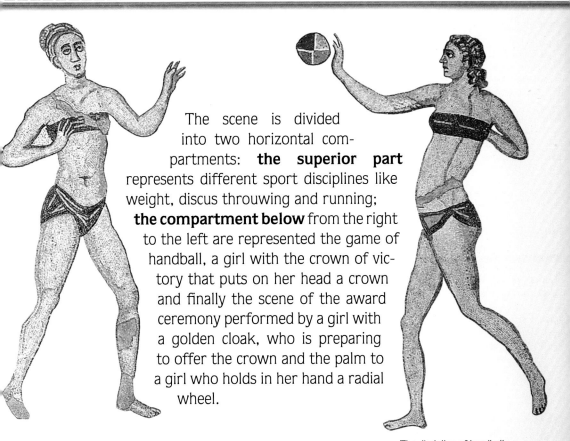

The scene is divided into two horizontal compartments: **the superior part** represents different sport disciplines like weight, discus throuwing and running; **the compartment below** from the right to the left are represented the game of handball, a girl with the crown of victory that puts on her head a crown and finally the scene of the award ceremony performed by a girl with a golden cloak, who is preparing to offer the crown and the palm to a girl who holds in her hand a radial wheel.

The discipline of handball.

The scene of the ceremony. Girl with palm and crown of victory twisted.

Statue of Apollo Liceo.

ROOM OF ORPHEUS

Along the peristyle is the entrance to the **room of Orpheus**, a rectangular room with a semicircular bottom, with a statue of **Apollo Liceo** a Roman copy of a greek original of Praxiteles. This room was for music auditions and on the foor is represented Orpheus, who plays the harp sitting on a stone.

The legend recalls that the poet with the sweet sound of his lyre was able to charm animalst that captured by the sublime music would run to him as an spellbound audience. In the mosaic are represented various animals from big ones such as elephants, hippos, camels and rhinos, to smaller ones

such as lizards, mice, birds, hedgehogs and snails.

By going through the ambulatory you can enter the courtyard orned by colymms that linked the private apartments to the triclinium and *xystus*.

Details of the mosaic animals enchanted by the sound of the lyre of Orpheus. Elephants, hippos, camels, peacocks, birds, lizards, snails, urchins.

THE TRICLINIUM

The **triclinium** was the large dining room where the dominus entertained importar guests. In this room there are three deep apses, where the couches were arranged which were beds, often made in bronze, but without backs but with cushions, on whic the diners, lying on side dined.

In the floor of this room are represented cults of Baccus and Hercules.

In the middle are represented

THE 12 LABOURS OF HERCULES:

1) The killing of the Nemean lion.
2) The Killing of the Hydra of Lerna monster with nine heads, eight mortal and one immortal.
3) The capture of the wild boar Erymanthian in a jar.
4) The Deer of Cyrene.
5) The Killing of Stinfalidi Birds.
6) Conquest of the girdle of the Amazon Hippolyta.
7) The cleaning of the Augean stables.
8) Capture of the Cretan bull.
9) Capture of the Mares of Diomedes King of Bistoni Knights.
10) The conquest of the oxens of Geryon, the monster with three bodies.
11) Conquest of Pomi Aurei (Golden apples).
12) Capture of the three-headed dog Cerberus.

Detail of a
Bistoni Knight.

Geryon The monster with three bodies.

In every corner of the rooms are represented some Bistoni Knight, killed by the arrows of Hercules. In the apses there are other mosaics. On the left the **glorification of Hercules** by Jupiter. You see the naked hero with powerful muscles and on his shoulders a leopard skin knotted on his chest to receive the laurel wreath on his head.

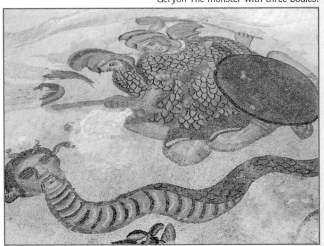

Killing Hydra.

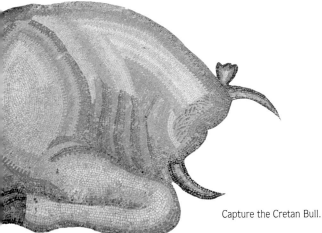

Capture the Cretan Bull.

Detail of a horse.

The mosaics that represented the metamorphosis of the **NYMPH DAPNE** into a laurel tree to **CYPARISSUS** in Cypress are also very beautiful.

The central part of the apse shows the **gigantomachy**, the story of the five giants who defied Zeus, and are killed by the poisoned arrows of Hercules dipped in the blood of the Hydra of Lerna, killed by the hero.

The giants, represented with snakes instead of feet, are depicted in the moment they pull the arrows from their body with a grimace of pain.

Below are shown **ESIONE** and **ENDIMIONE**.

Esione point to the sea monster from which she escape after it was killed from Endimione who at the same time that almost enchanted, point to the waning moon.

Metamorfosi di Dafne in piante di alloro e quella di Ciparisso in cipresso.

Glorification of Hercules by Jupiter.

Representing Esione and Endimione.

Gigantomachy - The five giants who had defied Jupiter, shot to death by poisoned arrows of Hercules dipped in the blood of the Hydra of Lerna.

Finally, the right abse is represented the **METAMORPHOSIS OF AMBROSIA**. The episode tells of the victory of the Dionysian powers against Lycurgus, king of Thrace. In the scene you see the Bacchante Ambrosia, who begins the metamorphosis, while the king Lycurgus, naked, tries to kill her with a hatchet axe. The branches of Ambrosia already bind the legs of Lycurgus, while a Dionysian procession seeks to defend the Bacchante. Beautiful is the scene of the satir lanches sacred panther on Lycurgus.

The scene represents the king Lycurgus who tries to kill Ambrosia.   Particular metamorphosis of Ambrosia.

Leaving the triclinium you access the "**XISTUS**", a large open ellipsoid atrium, which was used, perhaps, by the guests to have a walk after lavish lunches. The mosaics of the arcade depict busts of animals (tigers, lions, horses, wolves, geese, ducks, etc..) enclosed in acanthus leaves. There were several fountain to cheer up the guests. Around the courtyard there are a series of rooms where the guests would retire after meals in the company of girls skilled in the art of love, as well as in dances. The mosaics of these rooms represent cupids who cultivate the cupids, gather grapes and press grapes, while in the room of the vintage is also represented the bust of Dionysus, with a crown on the head. On the other hand, in the rooms, are represented cupids fishing. The other rooms contain remains of damaged mosaics. Beside the *xystus* there is a corridor that was used as connection between the peristyle and *xystus*, where there are mosaics representing animals and a vase with acanthus leaves, and then the kitchen where they prepared the food for receptions in the triclinium. On the opposite side of triclinium there is the aqueduct that supplies water to the basin, from which the water flewed to the various services till the fountain in the peristyle.

ust above there is the octagonal latrine, which served only the family of the dominus. The restaurant is in good condition, with frescoed walls and a mosaic representing a vase from which emerge branches of ivy. On the right there s a tank that fed the sewer. From here he tour continues through the rooms of domina. The first room is the "**DIAETA**" room) **OF ARION**, a large living room, where the landlady was used to listen music or chatting with the other membres

Room of Arion - A Nereid, Nymph.

of the family. The lunette of the room is represented the **GOD OCEAN**, with long thick hair, decorated with two claws, with the beard formed by marine plants and with the mouth from which exit the polyps, fish, shrimp and other sea creatures. Among other figures there is the poet Arion, who appears in the waves riding a dolphin, while playing the cither and the sea monster are around of him to form a ring around him, leaving the sea in the shape of griffins, tigers, panthers, wolves, ions, and oxen ridden by cute cupids. The mythological scene is complete with the Nereids, the water nimphs with theri elegant femininity, around Triton.

Xystus

Room of Arion - The Ocean God Triton with Cupids and sea animals.

Room of Arion - The Poet Airon in the waves riding a dolphin, while playing the cither.

Room of Arion - A Nereid with Tritorn.

Room of Arion - A Nereid, detail of mosaic dedicated to Arion on dolphin.

From this room you can visit the **VESTIBULE SEMI CIRCULAR**, a room with marble columns with ionic capitals.

The columms was in hemicycle holding up the *compluvium* (roof slopes to the internal), which collected the water, till the *impluvium* (tub).

This room was used to release the rooms of the children of *dominus* from the Dieta of Arion.

In the mosaics are winged cupids on boats while fishing with nets, traps and harpoons in a sea full of fish.

The following rooms are the four rooms of the children.
The first room is called **VESTIBU-LAR OF THE LITTLE CIRCUS**.

In the floor there are mosaics represented a race in the circus, where we can see the central spine with two tries, with chariots pulled by animals and led by children.

You can notice again that in the scene of the award of the winner the colors of the various factions represented the colors of the birds feathers.

Atrium vestibule Cupids winged boats while fishing with nets, traps and harpoons.

The small circus chariots pulled by animals and led by children.

Small Circus - The winner is awarded with the crown of victory.

The next room is the **CUBICLE OF MUSICIANS AND ACTORS** (the room of the daughter). In this room there was an apse with two columns, today missing, and on the floor you can see a scene of pagan festival of the goddess Flora (protector of flowering and of pregnant women), that was in spring.

You can see also two girls who weave wreaths of roses.

There is also a tree where you can notice a leaf of ivy, symbol of the family of Massimiano.

On the other side of the room there are other some mosaics arranged in three different levels.

In the mosaic on the top there are four performers of various musical instruments, and a figure with white robes and with palm in his hand as a reward for the winner. This man begins the musical competition raising his hand.

In the central part of the mosaic, between two male actors and two females, there is a large disk contening musical notes.

In the bottom of the scene there a group of people with long tunics and another disk with musical notes.

Cubicle of musicians and actors
Scene of the pagan festival
of the Goddess
Flora.

If you walk beyond the atrium, you can find other **two rooms**, symmetrical comparing the last two visited.

In the first room, the **VESTIBULE OF EROS AND PAN**, is represented the struggle between Pan, god of the woods, and Eros, the god of love.

On the left of Pan there is a referee with red cloak, a satyr and three menhaden. Behind Eros you can notice a group of spectators, that someone supposedly are the family of Massimiano. Over the two contenders is a *trapeza* (table supported by cables) rectangular, with four caps from Pannonia with palm branches, and below, there are two pockets with values.

On the pocket someone has written the figure of the amounts contained. Some studios think that this scene want describe the equity between the the two gods.

The struggle between Pan and Eros. A referee with red cloak.   In the right a group of spectators.

Cubicle of Children hunters - Girls gathering roses in baskets.

Cubicle of Children hunters - Boy with a pole carrying baskets overflowing with roses.

Cubicle of Children hunters - Young boyus engaged in hunting.

The second room is the **CUBICLE OF CHILDREN HUNTERS**, the son's room, where the mosaic scene is represented on three registers floral gender.

In the hight register there are girls who collect roses in baskets.

In the second one there is a young girl carrying baskets full of roses and in the opposite side of the mosaic there is another girl sitting on a basket weaves wreaths of roses.

In the lower register a child carrying a pole across his shoulders, with baskets overflowing with roses hung on eithe end.

Cubicle of Children hunters
Detail: boy catch a duck.

The rest of the floor registers are represented some young boys engaged in hunting.

In both, **the top register** and in the bottom one, there are guys hunting animals. In the middle you can notice, in the contrary, the animals that run after the boys. You can notice also a rooster biting a kneeling young boy.

Walking in the main marked route you arrive into **THE BASILICA**, surely the largest area of the villa, which leads to the ambulatory of the great huntig. In the Basilica the Emperor administered justice and oganized official receptions. On the walls of basilica you can see remains of the marble slabs that in the past adorned this area. On the floor there was all marble: there are remains of rotae in red porphyry and polychrome marbles, with palms and flowers. In the apse, raised above the rest of the floor, there was the imperial throne. Today you can see only the place where it was placed. At the center of the apse there was a gigantic statue of Hercules, which left only his head, storaged at the museum. Even in the entrance, located at the ambulatory of the great hunt, there were two great columns of red granite, supporting the architrave.

Cubicle of Children hunters - Rooster running after a young kneeling boy.

In this point you can visit the rooms of *dominus*, that lead the **VESTIBULE OF UIYSSES AND POLYPHEMUS.** The mosaic in this room is perhaps the most famous of the villa. In the mosaico is represented the episode of the Cyclops Polyphemus and Ulysses. Polyphemus is represented with three eyes, with beard and long hair. He is sitting on a large stone rock. Whit his left hand he holds a disembowled ram on his lap and with his right hand he takes the crater full of wine that the wily Odysseus, wearing a red tunich, has offered to him with the intention of making him drunk.

The next room is the **CUBICLE OF FRUIT**, the bedroom of domina, with an apse and walls decorated with frescoes, of which only a fragment remains, wiht a cupid. In the alcove the mosaics in the lunettes are with flowers, while in the rectangular room you can notice squares geometric area contain nine laurel wreaths with various types of fruit: figs, pomegranates, grapes, peaches, pears.

The last room is **A CUBICLE EROTIC SCENE**, the bedroom of dominus, consisting in two adjoining rooms.

The first place is one rectangular alcove, whose walls are frescoes representing a maenad and a satyr.

The mosaics in the bedroom floor you can recognize a four-petaled motif.

There is a strip dividing the room which depicts two young boys playing with balls in a circle and another side some other girls playing with balls in line.

Cubicle erotic scene
Female figures inside the hexagons,
which represent the four seasons.

Strip that separates the rooms. Two young men playing with balls in a circle and in the other side some girls playing with balls in line

he rest of the room is decorated with geometrical designs, masks and busts of
vomen. At the center of the room there is the famous medallion, a **dodecagon** with
 laurel wreath and with the **EROTIC SCENE** in which a young ephebe crowned
mbracing a young adolescent girl
vhile she is baring herself.

o the sides of dodeca-
on there are four
emale figures in-
ide hexagons, de-
icting the four
easons and
hen eight cir-
les containing
aurel wreaths
hat surround
emale theatrical
nasks.

ubicle erotic scene
he dodecagon. Particular where
young man embracing a young
dolescent girl while she is baring herself.

CITY ITINERARY

If you desire to know the city you have to start your itinerary from **Piazza Cascino**, where you can park your car and where there is the monument dedicated to General. Walking on Via Garibaldi on the right you will find the **theater** and the **Church of San Giovanni Battista,** today desecrated, built by the gerosolimitani Knights in gothic style. The portal, the windows and interior frescoes by Borremans are really very beautiful. On the left stands on a wide staircase, the **Church of Santo Stefano**. This Church has an hight façade articuleted by two side pilasters, and a little Baroque archade and in the top you can see three open arches for the bells. The walk continues through several palaces and churches till Piazza Garibaldi, real downtown, where facing the **Town Hall** and the **Church of San Rocco (church of Fundrò)**. Both monuments are build in the warm local sandstone and in the same style. Climbing the Via Vittorio Emanuele through magnificent buildings and churches, you will

Church of Santo Stefano.

Cascino square with monument to General.

Piazza Garibaldi with the Town Hall eighteenth century. On the right the church of San Rocco of the XVIII century.

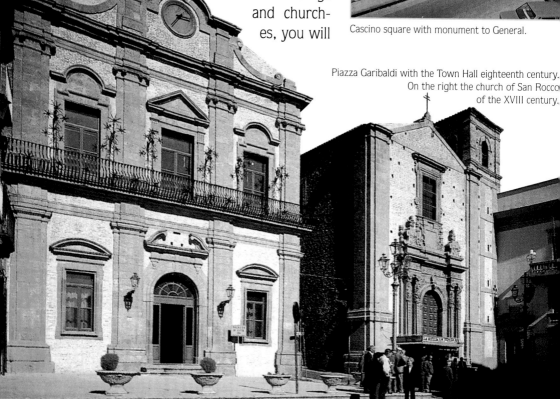

Aragonese Castle

Inside the cathedral.

Crucifix of the fifteenth century, by Antonello da Messina.

...ind the **Church of St. Ignatius** that is characterized by a beautiful staircase and the adjoining convent of the Jesuits. Almost opposite of St.Igntiius there is the monumental **Church of St. Anne** with convex front and arched windows.

Continuing our itineray we will arrive at quadrilateral **Aragonese Castle**, built in the XV centry, characterized by angular towers and bastions. The road ends on the esplanade of the **Piazza Duomo**, where, in addition to the major temple city, there is the magnificent **Palazzo Trigona**, with Baroque facade. The **Duomo**, that has a majestic dome that dominates the surrounding urban landscape, was built on a previous church, which traces can be seen in the first two orders of the original bell tower with magnificent windows in Gothic-Catalan, made of white limestone. The Duomo construction began in 1604, was completed in 1719 in typical Baroque style. Its magnificent carved portal takes the color of gold in the hours of sunset. In the majestic interior of the Duomo inside a nave are preserved works of art, as the picture with the Byzantine Madonna placed on the high altar, filled with polychrome marbles. It seems that this Madonna was a gift from Pope Nicholas II to Roger at the liberation of Sicily from the Arabs. Inside the Duomo are preserved some other works of art. At the entrance there is the tomb of Laura de Asaro; a beautiful arch in the baptistery, in the chapel on the left there is a magnificent sanctuary crucifix (1485) made from an unknown master from the Cross from Piazza Armerina and finally fine paintings and a rich treasure with various holy furnish and holy hangings.

The Duomo.

Church of St. Peter.

Priory of St. Andrew

In Piazza Armerina there are really many others monuments, magnificent palaces with baroque balconies supported by brackets and some churches, but many of them are badly preserved.

The strett and some area are particularly suggestive and rich of history. In Piazza Cascino you have to visit t the **Church of St. Peter** austere and rich church with celing chests and sculptures in Gagini's style. Near the church there is the entrance to the **Villa Comunale**, from whose hills you can enjoy sweeping views of the city. Out of town that is also worth a visit two other churches both for their history than for the artistic beauty. Near Armerino hill where stood the ancient city is the **Hermitage of Santa Maria della Platea** and the ancient **Priory of St. Andrew**, erected in 1096.

The gothic portals are wonderfull in both the façade and in the hips, and twelfth and thirteenth century frescoes in the interior walls.

Hermitage of Santa Maria della Platea.

FOLKLORE: THE PALIO OF NORMANNI

The Palio of Normanni it the greatest event during the folk festivals in Piazza Amerina. The Palio was established in 1952 and will be each year between 13 and 14 of August.

The event commemorates an event that dates back to the distant 1091, when the Great Count Roger gave to the town of Piazza Armerina the banner depicting the Holy Mary of Victories, who had received as gift as a good omens in the fight against the Saracens who held Sicily. The celebrations begin on 12 of August with the reading of the Public Announcement made on the streets of Pluto (Piazza Armerina), by an

auctioneer. The day aefter, 13 of August, is the commemoration of the entrance to the city of Count Roger, who accompanied by his troops on horseback and on foot, and his court, in the central Piazza del Duomo where is received the keys of the city. After this there is the parade, consisting of approximately 450 figures walking through the medieval streets.

The next day is devoted to the conduct of the Palio or Quintana, a competition between the four districts where the city is divided: Monte, Canale, Castellina and Casalotto. The knights with lance and mace must hit a target: the Moro. The team that totals the most points receives the Palio, the banner of the Lady of Victories, which will be kept throughout the year in the local church. Usually in the second half of May there is a special event and called "**Courtyards and blooming balconies**".

During the event all the balconies, courtyards and streets are decorated with flowers and plants. In Piazza Garibaldi a team of florists prepare a series of sketches of flowers, with scenes of local monuments. During these days there are many other cultural events, moreover, art exhibitions, handcrafts exhibitions and then flag wavers and some costumed groups make them shows.

Entrance into the city of Count Roger and his troops.

MUSEUM "THE VILLA DELLE MERAVIGLIE"
of ENZO CAMMARATA

At about 300 meters as the crow flies from the famous Villa Romana del Casale where you can admire the mosaics of the late imperial era of the most beautiful in the world declared from Unesco Heritage, there is,inside a seventeenth century villa, a valuable museum, built by Enzo Cammarata and inaugureted in October 2008. Since the half of the XIX century, the Cammarata family members, as was used in the past in some other noble families, guided by love for the beauty, and by the sense of hospitality to foreign travelers, and guided also by ties of friendship and correspondence with the dense relations with european studious of art and the science, picked up and collected antique furniture and objects of great value and rarity.

The anchestor of the family was Domenico Cammarata, erudite person born in Piazza Armerina in the half of XIX century, who starting this collection. After him with great passion for the ancient cultures, and helped from his wife Agatha, Enzo incresed and created a great and worthy collection with valuable historical and artistic importance. The museum, contains not only furniture dating from the Renaissance to the eighteenth century, but also furniture from the neo-classicism and throughout the nineteenth century. In the museium are exhibited some medioeval ceramics from various eras; you can find remains of Roman sculptures and subsequent periods, paintings, beautiful micro-mosaics, collections of marble and semiprecious stones, some carved wood objects, some beautiful works of Oriental art, and even collections of books, prints, bronzes, all items attributable to the various cultures that have been linked

Windows with a display of Renaissance majolica and parade armor in the exhibition halls of the Museum Enzo Cammarata.

Crater glass penthouse - Ceramics in red paint
Representation of a satyr chasing a maenad - XIX century

Marble group "Hercules baby out with the goose"
Marble - XVI century.

at various times with the rich soil of Sicily. Among the fine furniture that will attrack the attention of visitors, there is a lounge style Louis XV, two crescent windows in Louis XIV 's style made by wood in Rome, a lectern for the choir of the XVIII century, a coin cabinet with cantilever ivory sculptures applications and among the most important artistic head of a child attributed to Francesco Laurana and a marble group representing Hercules baby wiht a goose, attributed to Michelangelo; you can find also a painted majolica representing a Madonna with Child of Luca della Robbia and a bell-shaped crater with red figures, with the image of Hercules slaying the centaur Nessos in one hand and, and on the other side, a satyr chasing a maenad. After this room in the so-called "noble floor" there are some other rooms full of pieces of particular importance that lend their names to them. Connected by a marble staircase there is the upper floor, with other rooms decorated with majolica pieces and then still a beautiful bedroom with antiques furniture. The museum has all the facilities for the reception of groups who choose to spend a pleasant day in Piazza Armerina in a context and environment of exceptional quality.

The visit to the museum charges during the opening time:
– in summer from 9.00 to 19.00
– in winter from 9.00 to 17.00.
Info: Villa delle Meraviglie
C/da Casale - 94015 Piazza Armerina
Tel/Fax +39.0935.689055
www.villadellemeraviglie.it
e-mail: info@villadellemeraviglie.it

"Head of a Child" - Marble Sicily, second half XV century
The attribution to Francesco Laurana (1430 - 1502).

The territory of Piazza Armerina offers the possibility of different natural walks, in the fresh air from the woods and give you the opportuny to know considerable flora and fauna of this area. Among the routes we can suggest the Park of Ronza and R.N.O. Rossomanno Grottascura Bellia.

PARK OF RONZA

Park of Ronza is a green area which is located about 5 km from the town, along the of Enna's main road. The area that is part of the demesne of the biggest Rossomano Grottascura Bellia, is managed by the Forester. This territory, that is protected and fenced, during the warmer months becomes popular beacuse offers cool and for the possibility of long walks, during which you may encounter fallow deer, buck. wild boar and various species of birds. In the Park, during the spring flowering, you can find many spieces of plants like the iris, the marigolds, and various species of graminaceous, many kind of three like eucalyptus, pines, locust, pear, ampelodesma, euphorbia and other typical species of Mediterranean flora. The park offers for free service some barbecue, cut firewood and water's fountains for wonderful picnics.

R.N.O. ROSSOMANO GROTTASCURA BELLIA

In 2000 the territory of Enna, Piazza Armerina and Aidone becomes a reserve. This reserve is very rich of nature; there infact grows some eucalyptus and domestic pines, but there are also pear-tree, rowans, oaks, chestnut trees and thick brushwood. One of the tasks of the Company State Forests is to restore the original oak forest, thinning the allochthonous species (eucalyptus). Entering the gate of the equipped area called Ronza, along the main road n.117, you will find the largest picnic areas with benches, tables and cooking points, and besides Wild Fauna Recovery Center. Inside the Park there are also the "enchanted stones" or "puppet dancers", that are the result of percolation of water rich of calcium in the sand that is podologic the podooigic substrate contrary to the legend that narretes that this people were petrified during a sabbatical dance.

AIDONE AND THE MORGANTINA VENUS

This city is located about 10 km from the Reserve. The city, with his ancient origins, take her name from the hight hill (850 meter above see level).

The name Aidone seems arrives from the Arabic root "Ayn-Dun" that means "higher source", a name which the Arabs had given to that place because was so rich of water. Settlers Lombard that were arrived beside Normans in Sicily, after winning the Arabs, had chosen this airy hill as new residence. The Arabic root was crippled in the Lombard dialect in "Aydon" so becomes the actual name Aidone.

Certainly the first nucleus of the city was formed in the XII century between the mighty castle and the rich priory of Santa Maria la Cava. The city, in a strategic position, was sought after during the feudal period. A tour in the old core of Aidone gives us the opportunity to discover an urban plan, despite the inevitable changes, that retain the typica medieval structur wiith Islamic influences (narrow alleys and courtyards).

The Archaeological Museum, a deconsecrated church, houses the Morgantina Venus, a famous 5th century BC Greek sculpture which was returned to the town after having been looted by tomb raiders in the late 1970s. Among the important monuments of this area you may notice the original ashlar facade a "diamond" of

The Morgantina Venus

Church of San Domenico of 1419 with a facade a "diamond".

the **Church of San Domenico**, and the frescoes that adorn the ceiling of the **Church of Santa Maria della Cava**, built on a former temple with Norman origins. In this church in the night of 1st of May thousands pilgrims arrive walking on foot and often barefoot after several kilometers to pay homage to St. Filippo Neri.

At a distance of 4 km from Aidone in locality Serra Orlando, on the Erei mountain plateau, in a most agreeable place you will find the ancient and picturesque city of Morgantina. The excavations at Morgantina revealed a village of ancient origin, whose original inhabitants were the supposed Morgeti, an Italic people which together with the Sicilians and in different periods have arrived in the south of Italy in prehistoric times, forcing Sicani living in these territories to move to the west coast of Sicily. Traces of this period are in the area of San Francesco and the Cittadella where you can find the remains of huts with circular or rectangular fondations.

In the eighty century B.C. arrived in this area the Greeks, who after the establishment of several coastal towns begin an expansion inwards and reaching Morgantina. The Grekks mingled with the natives and started to organize a real city with the characteristics of the Greek polis. This first city, which is one of the best examples of centers of Hellenized Sicily area, was destroyed several times but always rebuilt. The first time was destroyed by Hippocrates of Gela (500 B.C.), who wanted to submit all the Greek colonies as Morgantina, and later by Sicilian community (Siculi, Morgeti, Sicani) who had joined forces under the leadership of Ducezio against the Greek policy expansion.

After the defeat of Ducezio a Nome in 450 B.C., the dream of independence of Sicily was never realized. When after the struggles between Syracuse and Athens in

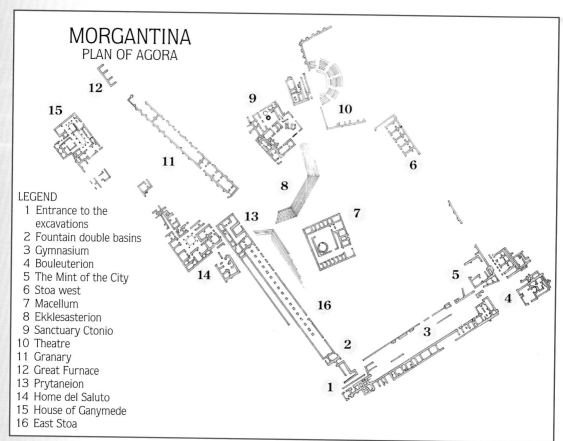

MORGANTINA
PLAN OF AGORA

LEGEND
1 Entrance to the excavations
2 Fountain double basins
3 Gymnasium
4 Bouleuterion
5 The Mint of the City
6 Stoa west
7 Macellum
8 Ekklesasterion
9 Sanctuary Ctonio
10 Theatre
11 Granary
12 Great Furnace
13 Prytaneion
14 Home del Saluto
15 House of Ganymede
16 East Stoa

427 B.C. was proclaimed the autonomy of the cities of Sicily from mainland Greece, Morgantina was assigned to Camarina upon payment of a sum of dracme. During this period (IV century B.C.) in the city were built various civil, political and religious monuments and defensive walls. Then with Agathocles, tyrant of Syracuse, were placed the agora and shrines of chthonic deities (Demetra and Kore), was built and the new Greek quarter.

Morgantina during this period of glory was the only city of Sicily, that issues currency. But when the city rebelled against Rome during the Punic Wars, the consul Claudio Marcello destroyed it and gave Morgantina to the auxiliary Spaniards that were with the Romans. Morgantina in this period issues Spanish coins. Some archaelogists from this founded coins identifyed the site of Serra Orlando with the city of Morgantina. When Sicily became a Roman province, the city was classified decumana.

For this reason Rome obtain the payment of the 20% of the harvest, that means a double tithe. Morgantina was destroyed when during the civil wars it ranged against Octavian and for this reason the site was abandoned.

Strabone speaks of the beginning of the imperial age about Morgantina as a city that "once time existed, but that does not exist more."

Entrance to the excavations.

VISIT OF THE ARCHAEOLOGICAL AREA

Entering on site you will find "**THE AGORA**", a large open space surrounded on his three sides by arcades long 100 meters. This place one time was a vital center of social life.

These arcades (stoai) that had the columns in the external sides and inside some pillars, of which there still are only some remains, and that supported a gabled roof, had different functions: those on the east side was for political activities, those on the west side were used for the trading, with some shops opened on the Agora.

The arcades on the north side certainly was used as a "**gymnasium**", a place

Gymnasium.

used for sporting activities. In the last few arcades during the Roman period were obtained a few rooms for shops. At the entrance there is a large fountain with two basins. This fountain, fed by a spring, was certainly an important meeting point where anyone can drink and find water for domestic uses.

The square, with its gently sloping floor, was divided in two part by a **trapezoidal staircase** with fifteen steps, with different functions: one area for the politic and the other one for commercial and religious activities. The staircase, which is a beautiful architectural backdrop, was used as "**Ekklesiasterion**" (the place for city meetings), with an adjacent "**bema**", the stone pedestal from where the orators make them speechs. Next to the Gymnasium there is an quadrangula environment called the "**bouleuterion**" used for the meetings of the Senate of the city. The Senate was the most important organ of the community with legislative, executive and judicial functions. Next there is a "**taberna**", a kind of modern bar used to sell wines. You can still see the stone seats and some supports for the table.

Ekklesiasterion.

Bouleterium area.

Further north there is the "**macellum**", ample space for the sale of food.
You can still see some shops surrounding the courtyard with arcades.
In the center of macellum there is a arcade with structure a *tolos* that we dont know
for what was used for.

Sanctuario Ctonio.

In the entrance of the market you can notice two rooms that contained the statues of the deities that protected the market.

Little further there is an environment consisting of two rectangular areas: it is the **Santuario Ctonio** gods for the earth (Demetra Proserpina and Kore or Cerere).

This area was surrounded

Macellum.

by a *temenos* wall and included some altars and also a furnace for the production of terracotta votive statuettes. There's still a circular enclosure containing a cylindrical altar, on which rested the statue of the goddess. All the clay busts of gods and votive offerings foundend in Morgantina arived from this sacred area.

Even the nearby **theater dates from about the fourth century B.C.** and could hold up to 5000 spectators. The theater, located on the hillside, was built and not carved in the rock, like so many other theaters in Sicily were. The theater has an auditorium lying on the artificial bank, held in place by thick walls and internal buttresses The auditorium is divided by five vertical scales and six radial sectors. Each sector of the auditorium was dedicated to a god, in fact from above the third step you can be read a dedication to Archelao, son of the god Dionisio and Eukleide. Every year, thanks to the special acoustic and the commitment of the Province of Enna and the Capua Antica Festival, in summer this theater back to relive his superb, hosting performances from classical circuit National "*Teatri di pietra*".

On the opposite side of agora there is a long building with large rooms of different sizes. Someones supposed that was the warehouses used for storage grain and cereals, perhaps the **public granary** for the storage of wheat reserved for taxes to Rome before and after to Syracuse. In the lower part there are two **furnaces**. About one of them you can see the tunnel where was burning firewood and cooking the bricks for construction purposes. In the eastern part of the agora, before the first residential neighborhood, there is a rectangular room, a public building that is supposedly the "**pritaneo**" (prytaneion), meeting pont for judges and host for famous people. Slopes in the east and west side there are residential areas, and right next to prytaneum, there is the **Home del Saluto**, also known as **Home**

Mosaic - Rape of Ganimede.

of the **Doric capital** because there is a mosaic "**EYEXE**" (a wish of good healf). In this building thre is a columned portico,were discovered earthenware floors with mosaics.

Just behind is the **Home of Ganimede**, one of the most elegant abode in Morgantina. The building has a rectangular peristyle, which, with seven columns on the long sides and three on the short sides, surrounding a courtyard to collect rainwater. There is an environment that gives the name to the house. There is infact a a mosaic depicting the **Rape of Ganimede**, while on the walls there are still traces of red plaster.

The number of houses that can be visited all denote social status attained by the owner. Among them the **House of the bow tank**, one of the largest and most luxurious homes Morgantina where there are still some rooms with beautiful mosaics, the **Home golden currency**, the **Home of antefisse**, the **Home of tuscani capitals**, the **House of the magistrate**. Some houses, belonging definitely to noble owners, have some environments with mosaic floors or earthenware in which many different designs, inspired by geometric or natural patterns, are evidence of mastery of the craftsmen of this time.

You can find also some ruins of the **House of Eupolemo**, where they were looted a rich and unique collection of silver, which are currently at the Museum of New York and finally in 2010 came back in Morgantina.

Theatre.

EDITION

© Copyright 2011 by
OGB Officina Grafica Bolognese S.r.l.
Via A. Pollastri, 22 - 40138 Bologna - Italia
Tel. +39 051 532 203 - Fax +39 051 532 188
e-mail: info@ogbsrl.it - www.ogbsrl.it
Printed in UE by OGB Officina Grafica Bolognese S.r.l. - Bologna - Italy
Text: Giuseppe Iacono
Pictures by: Archivio OGB
Printing completed in March 2011
ISBN: 9788860781413

Distributor: Parisi Antonino
Tel. +39 091 7630526 - Fax +39 091 5087948
e-mail: turisticamenteparisi@libero.it
www.parisisouvenir.it